In the Year 1923

by

Kerry Butters.

In the Year 1923

Millennium: 2nd millennium

Centuries: 19th century – **20th century** – 21st century

Decades: 1890s 1900s 1910s – 1920s – 1930s 1940s 1950s

Years: 1920 1921 1922 – **1923** – 1924 1925 1926

1923 (MCMXXIII) was a common year starting on Monday (dominical letter G) of the Gregorian calendar and a common year starting on Sunday (dominical letter A) of the Julian calendar, the 1923rd year of the Common Era (CE) and *Anno Domini* (AD) designations, the 923rd year of the 2nd millennium, the 23rd year of the 20th century, and the 4th year of the 1920s decade. Note that the Julian day for 1923 is 13 calendar days difference, which continued to be used from 1582 until the complete conversion of the Gregorian calendar was entirely done in 1929.

Contents

Events

January

- January 1 – The Grouping: All major British railway companies are grouped into four larger companies, under terms of the Railways Act 1921.
- January 1–7 – Rosewood massacre, a violent, racially motivated conflict in Florida. At least eight people are killed, and the town of Rosewood is abandoned and destroyed.
- January 9 – Lithuania begins the Klaipėda Revolt to annex the Klaipėda Region (Memel Territory).
- January 11 – Despite strong British protests, troops from France and Belgium occupy the Ruhr area to force Germany to make reparation payments.
- January 17 – Juan de la Cierva invents the autogyro, a rotary-winged aircraft with an unpowered rotor.

- January 18 – Elon College's campus in North Carolina is destroyed by a fire.

February

- Norman Albert calls the first live broadcast of an ice hockey game, the third period of an Ontario Hockey League Intermediate playoff game on the Toronto station CFCA.
- February 9 – Billy Hughes resigns as Prime Minister of Australia, after the Country Party refuses to govern in coalition with him as the leader of the Nationalist Party. Hughes is succeeded by his Treasurer, Stanley Bruce.
- February 23 – Albert Einstein visits Barcelona, Spain, at the invitation of scientist Esteban Terradas i Illa.

March

- March 1
  - The USS *Connecticut* is decommissioned.
  - Greece adopts the Gregorian calendar.
- March 3 – This is the cover date of the first issue of *Time* magazine. Retired U.S. Speaker of the House Joseph G. Cannon appears on the first cover.
- March 6 – The Egyptian Feminist Union (Arabic: الاتحاد النسائي المصري), the first nationwide feminist movement in Egypt, was founded at the home of activist Huda Sha'arawi.

- March 9 – Vladimir Lenin suffers his third stroke, which renders him bedridden and unable to speak; consequently he retires from his position as Chairman of the Soviet government.
- March 14 – Pete Parker calls the play-by-play of the first ice hockey game ever broadcast on the radio in its entirety, between the Regina Capitals and the Edmonton Eskimos of the Western Canada Hockey League.
- March 28 – *Regia Aeronautica*, the air force of Fascist Italy, is founded.

April

- April 4 – Warner Bros. film studio is formally incorporated in the United States as Warner Brothers Pictures, Inc.
- April 6
  - Louis Armstrong makes his first recording, "Chimes Blues", with King Oliver's Creole Jazz Band.
  - The first Prefects Board in Southeast Asia is formed in Victoria Institution, Federated Malay States.
- April 12 – Kandersteg International Scout Centre comes into existence in Switzerland.

- April 18 – Yankee Stadium opens its doors as the home park of the New York Yankees baseball team in The Bronx.
- April 19
  - Hjalmar Branting leaves office as Prime Minister of Sweden, after the Swedish Riksdag has rejected a government proposal regarding unemployment benefits.
  - Right-wing academic and jurist Ernst Trygger becomes Prime Minister of Sweden.
- April 19 – Egyptian Constitution of 1923 adopted, introducing a parliamentary system of democracy in the country.
- April 23 – The Gdynia seaport is inaugurated on the Polish Corridor.
- April 26 – Prince Albert, Duke of York (later George VI, King of the United Kingdom) marries Lady Elizabeth Bowes-Lyon (later Queen Elizabeth The Queen Mother) in Westminster Abbey.
- April 28 – The original Wembley Stadium opened its doors for the first time to the British public staging the FA Cup Final between Bolton Wanderers and West Ham Utd.

May

- May 1 – Rahula College is established in Ceylon with the name of "Parakramabhahu Vidyalaya".

- May 8 – Liseberg, an amusement park in Gothenburg, Sweden, opens.
- May 9
  - Southeastern Michigan receives a record 15 centimetres (5.9 in) of snow after temperatures plummeted from 17 to 1 degrees between 1 and 6 pm on the previous day.
  - The premiere of Bertolt Brecht's play *In the Jungle (Im Dickicht)* at the Residenztheater in Munich is interrupted by Nazi demonstrators.
- May 23 – Belgium's *Sabena* Airlines is created.
- May 24 – The Irish Civil War ends.
- May 26 – The first 24 Hours of Le Mans motor race is held, and is won by André Lagache and René Léonard.
- May 27 – The Ku Klux Klan in the United States defies a law requiring publication of its members.

June

- June 9 – A military coup in Bulgaria ousts prime minister Aleksandar Stamboliyski (he is killed June 14).
- June 12 – William Walton's *Façade* is performed for the first time.
- June 13 – President Li Yuanhong of China abandons his residence because a warlord has commanded forces to surround the mansion and cut off its water

and electric supplies, in order to force him to abandon his post.

- June 16 – The storming of Ayan in Siberia concludes the Yakut Revolt and the Russian Civil War.
- June 18 – Mount Etna erupts in Italy, making 60,000 homeless.
- June 25 – FC Rapid București is formed on the initiative of the Grivița railroad workers (first named CFR București).

July

- July 10 – Large hailstones kill 23 in Rostov, Soviet Union.
- July 13 – The Hollywood Sign is inaugurated in California (originally reading *Hollywoodland*).
- July 13 – American explorer Roy Chapman Andrews discovers the first dinosaur eggs near Flaming Cliffs, Mongolia.
- July 20 – Pancho Villa is assassinated at Hidalgo del Parral, Chihuahua.
- July 24 – The Treaty of Lausanne, settling the boundaries of the modern Republic of Turkey, is signed in Switzerland by Greece, Bulgaria and other countries that fought in the First World War, bringing an end to the Ottoman Empire after 624 years.
- *Undated* – Hyperinflation in Germany has seen the number of marks needed to purchase a single

American dollar reach 353,000 - more than 200 times the amount needed at the start of the year.

August

- August 2 – U.S. President Warren G. Harding, dies of a heart attack and is succeeded by Vice President Calvin Coolidge as President of the United States.
- August 13
  - The first major seagoing ship arrives at Gdynia, the newly constructed Polish seaport.
  - Gustav Stresemann is named Chancellor of Germany and founds a coalition government for the Weimar Republic, where hyperinflation means that more than 4,600,000 marks are now needed to buy a single American dollar.
- August 21 – Necaxa football club is founded by engineer William H. Frasser.
- August 30 – Hurricane season begins, with a tropical storm northeast of the Turks and Caicos Islands.
- August 31 – The Italian navy occupies Corfu in retaliation for the murder of an Italian officer. The League of Nations protests and the occupation ends on September 30.

September

- September 1 – The Great Kantō earthquake devastates Tokyo and Yokohama, killing an estimated 142,807 people, but according to a Japanese construction research center report in 2005, 105,000 are confirmed dead.

- September 4 – The United States Navy's first home-built rigid airship USS *Shenandoah* (ZR-1) makes her first flight at Naval Air Station Lakehurst (New Jersey); she contains most of the world's extracted reserves of helium at this time.
- September 7 – At the International Police Conference in Vienna, the International Criminal Police Commission (ICPC), better known as Interpol, is set up.
- September 8 – Honda Point disaster: Nine United States Navy destroyers run aground off the California coast.
- September 9 – Turkish head of state Mustafa Kemal Atatürk founds the Republican People's Party (CHP).
- September 10 – The Irish Free State joins the League of Nations.
- September 13 – Military coup in Spain: Miguel Primo de Rivera takes over, setting up a dictatorship. Trade unions are prohibited for 10 years.
- September 17 – 1923 Berkeley Fire: A major fire in Berkeley, California, erupts, consuming some 640 structures, including 584 homes in the densely built neighborhoods north of the campus of the University of California.

- September 18–26 – Newspaper printers strike in New York City.
- September 24 – Second storm of the Atlantic hurricane season, a major hurricane north of Hispaniola.
- September 26 – In Bavaria, Gustav Ritter von Kahr takes dictatorial powers.
- September 29 – The British Mandate for Palestine (1922) comes into effect, officially creating the protectorates of Palestine as a homeland for the Jewish people under British administration and Transjordan as a separate emirate under Abdullah I.
- September 29 – The French Mandate for Syria and the Lebanon takes effect.
- September 30 – Küstrin Putsch: Outside Berlin, Major Ernst von Buchrucker, the leader of the Black Reichswehr attempts a *putsch* by seizing several forts.

October

Oct.29: Kemal Atatürk.

- October 2 – After two days of siege, Major Buchrucker and his men surrender.
- October 6 – The great powers of World War I withdraw from Constantinople.
- October 13
  - Ankara replaces Constantinople as the capital of Turkey.
  - The first recorded example of a storm crossing from the Eastern Pacific into the Atlantic, occurred in Oaxaca.
- October 14 – Fourth tropical storm of the year, formed just north of Panama.
- October 15 – Fifth tropical storm of the year, formed north of the Leeward Islands.
- October 16
  - A sixth tropical storm develops in the Gulf of Mexico; a rare occurrence, it consists of four active tropical storms simultaneously.
  - Roy and Walt Disney found The Walt Disney Company.
- October 23 – Hamburg Uprising: In Germany, the Communists attempt a "putsch" in Hamburg, which results in street battles in that city for the next two days, when it ends unsuccessfully.
- October 26 – In Persia, Reza Khan becomes Ahmad Shah Qajar's prime minister.
- October 27 – In Germany, General Hans von Seeckt orders the *Reichswehr* to dissolve the Social

Democratic-Communist government of Saxony, which is refusing to accept the authority of the *Reich* government.

- October 29 – Turkey becomes a republic following the dissolution of the Ottoman Empire. Kemal Atatürk is elected as first president.
- October 30 – İsmet İnönü is appointed as the first prime minister of Turkey.

November

- November 1 – The Finnish flag carrier Finnair airline is started in Aero Oy.
- November 8 – Beer Hall Putsch: In Munich, Adolf Hitler leads the Nazis in an unsuccessful attempt to overthrow the Bavarian government; police and troops crush the attempt the next day.
- November 11 – Adolf Hitler is arrested for his leading role in the Beer Hall Putsch, two days after the Putsch was crushed by the government. 20 people died as a result of the associated violence.
- November 12 – Her Highness Princess Maud of Fife marries Captain Charles Alexander Carnegie in Wellington Barracks, London.
- November 15 – Hyperinflation in the Weimar Republic: Hyperinflation in Germany reaches its height. One United States dollar is worth 4,200,000,000,000 Papiermark (4.2 trillion on the short

scale). Gustav Stresemann abolishes the old currency and replaces it with the Rentenmark at an exchange rate of one Rentenmark to 1,000,000,000,000 (one trillion on the short scale) Papiermark with effect from November 20.

- November 23 – Gustav Stresemann's coalition government collapses in Germany.

December

- December 10 – Sigma Alpha Kappa (the first social fraternity at a Jesuit college in the United States) is founded as a fraternal organization until the ban on social fraternities is lifted.
- December 12 – In Italy, the Po River dam bursts, killing 600.
- December 20 – BEGGARS Fraternity (the second social fraternity at a Jesuit college in the United States) is founded by nine men who have secured permission to do so from the Pope.
- December 21 – The Nepal–Britain Treaty is the first to define the international status of Nepal as an independent sovereign country.
- December 27 – The crown prince of Japan survives an assassination attempt in Tokyo.
- December 29 – Vladimir K. Zworykin files his first patent (in the United States) for "television systems".

Date unknown

- Struggling for a foothold in southern China, Sun Yat-sen decides to ally his Nationalist Kuomintang party with Comintern and the Communist Party of China.
- Johor–Singapore Causeway completed.
- Police strike in Australia.
- The American Law Institute is established.
- The Moderation League of New York becomes part of the movement for the repeal of Prohibition in the United States.
- Marcel Duchamp's artwork *The Bride Stripped Bare by Her Bachelors, Even* (*La mariée mise à nu par ses célibataires, même* or *The Large Glass*) is completed in the United States.
- Rainbow trout introduced into the upper Firehole River in Yellowstone National Park, United States.

Births

January

- January 1
    - Valentina Cortese, Italian actress
    - Vulo Radev, Bulgarian film director (d. 2001)
    - Roméo Sabourin, Canadian World War II spy (d. 1944)
- January 3 – Hank Stram, American football coach and broadcaster (d. 2005)
- January 5 – Sam Phillips, American record producer (d. 2003)
- January 6 – Jacobo Timerman, Argentine writer (d. 1999)
- January 7 – Hugh Kenner, Canadian literary critic (d. 2003)
- January 8
    - Larry Storch, American actor
    - Johnny Wardle, English cricketer (d. 1985)
- January 11 – Ernst Nolte, German historian
- January 12 – Ira Hayes, U.S. Marine flag raiser on Iwo Jima (d. 1955)
- January 15 – Lee Teng-hui, president of Taiwan and the "father of Taiwan's democracy"
- January 16
    - Anthony Hecht, American poet (d. 2004)
    - Walther Wever, German fighter ace (d. 1945)

- January 19 – Jean Stapleton, American actress (d. 2013)
- January 20
  - Slim Whitman, American country and western musician (d. 2013)
  - Nora Brockstedt, Norwegian singer (d. 2015)
- January 22 – Diana Douglas, British-born American actress; mother of actor/producer Michael Douglas (d. 2015)
- January 23
  - Cot Deal, American major league baseball player and coach (d. 2013)
  - Stephanie Kwolek, inventor of "Kevlar fibers" (d. 2014)
- January 25 – Arvid Carlsson, Swedish scientist, recipient of the Nobel Prize in Physiology or Medicine
- January 26 – Anne Jeffreys, American actress and singer
- January 29 – Paddy Chayefsky, American writer (d. 1981)
- January 31 – Norman Mailer, American writer and journalist (d. 2007)

February

- February 2
    - James Dickey, American poet and author (*Deliverance*) (d. 1997)
    - Liz Smith, American gossip columnist
    - Clem Windsor, Australian rugby union player and surgeon (d. 2007)
- February 3 – Edith Barney, American female professional baseball player (d. 2010)
- February 4 – Conrad Bain, Canadian-born actor (d. 2013)
- February 7 – George Lascelles, 7th Earl of Harewood and first grandchild of King George V (d. 2011)
- February 9 – Brendan Behan, Irish author (d. 1964)
- February 10
    - Allie Sherman, American professional football coach (d. 2015)
    - Cesare Siepi, Italian opera singer (d. 2010)
- February 12 – Franco Zeffirelli, Italian film and opera director
- February 13
    - Yfrah Neaman, Lebanese-born violinist (d. 2003)
    - Chuck Yeager, American test pilot and *NASA* official
- February 16 – Samuel Willenberg, Polish-born Israeli sculptor and painter, last surviving member of the Treblinka extermination camp revolt (d. 2016)

- February 17 – Jun Fukuda, Japanese film director (d. 2000)
- February 20 – Forbes Burnham, President of Guyana (d. 1985)
- February 21 – Wilbur R. Ingalls, Jr., American architect (d. 1997)
- February 22 – Norman Smith, English singer and record producer (d. 2008)
- February 23 – Mary Francis Shura, American writer (d. 1991)
    - Ioannis Grivas, Greek judge and politician, 176th Prime Minister of Greece
    - John van Hengel, American "Father of Food Banking" (d. 2005)
- February 24 – David Soyer, American cellist (d. 2010)
- February 27 – Dexter Gordon, American jazz saxophone player (d. 1990)
- February 28
    - Jean Carson, American actress (d. 2005)
    - Charles Durning, American actor (d. 2012)

March

- March 2 – Orrin Keepnews, American record producer (d. 2015)
- March 3 – Doc Watson, American folk guitarist and songwriter (d. 2012)
- March 4

- Sir Patrick Moore, British astronomer and broadcaster (d. 2012)
  - Piero D'Inzeo, Italian Olympic show jumping rider (d. 2014)
- March 6
  - Ed McMahon, American television personality (d. 2009)
  - Wes Montgomery, American musician (d. 1968)
- March 7 – Mahlon Clark, American musician (d. 2007)
- March 8 – Louk Hulsman, Dutch criminologist (d. 2009)
- March 9
  - James L. Buckley, American politician and United States Senator 1971-77
  - Walter Kohn, Austrian-born physicist, recipient of the Nobel Prize in Chemistry (d. 2016)
- March 10 – Val Logsdon Fitch, American nuclear physicist, Nobel Prize laureate (d. 2015)
- March 11 – Paul Muller, Swiss actor
- March 12
  - Hjalmar Andersen, Norwegian speed-skater (d. 2013)
  - Wally Schirra, American astronaut (d. 2007)
  - Mae Young, American wrestler (d. 2014)
- March 14 – Diane Arbus, American photographer (d. 1971)
- March 21

- Merle Keagle, American female professional baseball player (d. 1960)
- Shri Mataji Nirmala Srivastava, Indian founder of Sahaja Yoga (d. 2011)
- March 22 – Marcel Marceau, world-renowned French mime (d. 2007)
- March 24
  - Murray Hamilton, American actor (d. 1986)
  - Michael Legat, English writer (d. 2011)
- March 25 – Wim van Est, Dutch cyclist (d. 2003)
- March 26 – Bob Elliott, American comedian (d. 2016)
- March 27 – Louis Simpson, Jamaican-born poet (d. 2012)
- March 28 – Thad Jones, American jazz musician (d. 1986)
- March 29 – Geoff Duke, British motorcycle racer (d. 2015)
- March 30 – Milton Acorn, Canadian writer (d. 1986)
- March 31 – Shoshana Damari, Yemenite-Israeli singer (d. 2006)

April

Aaron Spelling

- April 2
  - Alice Haylett, American professional baseball player (d. 2004)
  - G. Spencer-Brown, British mathematician
  - Gloria Henry, American actress
  - Johnny Paton, Scottish football player, coach and manager (d. 2015)
- April 4
  - Peter Vaughan, English actor
  - Gene Reynolds, Anerican actor
- April 6 – Ramón Valdés, Mexican comedian (d. 1988)
- April 8
  - George Fisher, American political cartoonist (d. 2003)
  - Edward Mulhare, Irish-born American actor (d. 1997)
- April 13 – Don Adams, American actor and comedian (d. 2005)
- April 14 – Roberto De Vicenzo, Argentine professional golfer and winner of the 1967 Open Championship
- April 20
  - Mother Angelica, American nun; founder of the Eternal Word Television Network (EWTN) (d. 2016)
  - Irene Lieblich, Polish-born painter (d. 2008)
- April 22

- Geoffrey Hattersley-Smith, English/Canadian geologist and glaciologist (d. 2012)
- Bettie Page, American model (d. 2008)
- Aaron Spelling, American television producer and writer (d. 2006)
- April 23 – Dolph Briscoe, Governor of Texas (d. 2010)
- April 25 – Albert King, American musician (d. 1992)
- April 30
  - Al Lewis, American actor (*The Munsters*) (d. 2006)
  - Francis Tucker, South African Rally Driver (d. 2008)

May

Anne Baxter

Heydar Aliyev

Horst Tappert

Henry Kissinger

Rainier III, Prince of Monaco

- May 1 – Joseph Heller, American novelist (*Catch-22*) (d. 1999)
- May 2 – Patrick Hillery, President of Ireland (d. 2008)
- May 3 – Ralph Hall, American politician
- May 4
    - Assi Rahbani, Lebanese composer, musician, conductor, poet and author (d. 1986)

- Eric Sykes, English actor (d. 2012)
- May 5 – Richard Wollheim, English philosopher (d. 2003)
- May 7 – Anne Baxter, American actress (d. 1985)
- May 10 – Heydar Aliyev, President of Azerbaijan (1993–2003) (d. 2003)
- May 11 – Louise Arnold, American female professional baseball player (d. 2010)
- May 15
  - Doris Dowling, American actress (d. 2004)
  - John Lanchbery, English composer (d. 2003)
- May 16 – Merton Miller, American economist, Nobel Prize laureate (d. 2000)
- May 18 – Hugh Shearer, Prime Minister of Jamaica (d. 2004)
- May 21
  - Armand Borel, Swiss mathematician (d. 2003)
  - Dorothy Hewett, Australian writer (d. 2002)
  - Evelyn Ward, American actress (d. 2012)
  - Ara Parseghian, American football coach
- May 23 – Kalidas Shrestha, Nepalese artist
- May 26
  - James Arness, American actor (d. 2011)
  - Roy Dotrice, English actor
  - Horst Tappert, German television actor (d. 2008)
- May 27 – Henry Kissinger, United States Secretary of State, recipient of the Nobel Peace Prize
- May 28

- György Ligeti, Hungarian composer (d. 2006)
- Nandamuri Taraka Rama Rao, Indian (Telugu) film actor (d. 1996)

- May 31
  - Robert O. Becker, American orthopedic surgeon (d. 2008)
  - Rainier III, Prince of Monaco (d. 2005)
  - Ellsworth Kelly, American artist (d. 2015)

June

- June 4 – Elizabeth Jolley, Australian writer (d. 2007)
- June 9 – Gerald Götting, German politician (d. 2015)
- June 10 – Robert Maxwell, Slovakian-born media entrepreneur (d. 1991)
- June 15 – Johnny Most, American basketball radio announcer (d. 1993)
- June 17 – Enrique Angelelli, Argentine bishop (d. 1976)
- June 20 – Bjørn Watt-Boolsen, Danish actor (d. 1998)
- June 23 – Giuseppina Tuissi, Italian Resistance fighter (d. 1945)
- June 25 – Sam Francis, American painter (d. 1994)
- June 27 – Gus Zernial, American baseball player and sports commentator (d. 2011)
- June 28 – Daniil Khrabrovitsky, Soviet film director (d. 1980)

July

- July 2 – Wisława Szymborska, Polish writer, Nobel Prize laureate (d. 2012)
- July 4 – Rudolf Friedrich, Swiss Federal Councilor (d. 2013)
- July 6 – Wojciech Jaruzelski, Polish Communist politician, Prime Minister and President of Poland (d. 2014)
- July 8 – Harrison Dillard, American athlete
- July 10 – John Bradley, U.S. Navy flag raiser on Iwo Jima (d. 1994)
- July 13
    - Alexandre Astruc, French film critic and director (d. 2016)
    - Norma Zimmer, American singer (d. 2011)
- July 18 – Jerome H. Lemelson, American inventor (d. 1997)
- July 20
    - Stanisław Albinowski, Polish economist and journalist (d. 2005)
    - Elisabeth Becker, German Nazi war criminal (d. 1946)
- July 21 – Rudolph A. Marcus, Canadian chemist, Nobel Prize laureate
- July 22
    - Bob Dole, American politician and Presidential candidate

- ○ The Fabulous Moolah, American professional wrestler (d. 2007)
- ○ Mukesh, Indian singer (d. 1976)
- July 23 – Witto Aloma, Cuban Major League Baseball player (d. 1997)
- July 25 – Estelle Getty, American actress (d. 2008)
- July 28 – H. S. S. Lawrence, Indian educator (d. 2009)
- July 29 – Jim Marshall, founder of Marshall Amplification (d. 2012)
- July 31 – Stephanie Kwolek, American chemist noted for inventing Kevlar (d. 2014)

August

Shimon Peres

Richard Attenborough

- August 2 – Shimon Peres, Prime Minister of Israel, President of Israel, recipient of the Nobel Peace Prize

- August 3
  - Jean Hagen, American actress (d. 1977)
  - Pope Shenouda III of Alexandria, Pope of the Coptic Orthodox Church of Alexandria (d. 2012)
- August 5
  - Sir Michael Kerry, QC, British civil servant, former Procurator General and Treasury Solicitor (d. 2012)
  - Devan Nair, third President of Singapore (d. 2005)
- August 6 – Moira Lister, Anglo-South African film, stage and television actress (d. 2007)
- August 10
  - Rhonda Fleming, American actress
  - Fred Ridgway, English cricketer (d. 2015)
- August 16 – Millôr Fernandes, Brazilian cartoonist and playwright (d. 2012)
- August 19 – Esmeralda Agoglia, Argentinian ballerina (d. 2014)
- August 20 – Jim Reeves, American country singer (d. 1964)
- August 21 – Larry Grayson, English comedian and game show host (d. 1995)
- August 23 – Henry F. Warner, American soldier, Medal of Honor (d. 1944)
- August 24 – Arthur Jensen, American educational psychologist (d. 2012)

- August 26 – Wolfgang Sawallisch, German conductor and pianist (d. 2013)
- August 27 – Hun Neang, father of Cambodian Prime Minister Hun Sen (d. 2013)
- August 29
  - Sir Richard Attenborough, English actor and film director (d. 2014)
  - Marmaduke Hussey, Baron Hussey of North Bradley, chairman of the BBC (d. 2006)
- August 30 – Giacomo Rondinella, Italian singer and actor (d. 2015)

September

- September 1
  - Rocky Marciano, American boxer (d. 1969)
  - Kenneth Thomson, Canadian businessman and art collector (d. 2006)
- September 4 – Ram Kishore Shukla, Indian Politician (d. 2003)
- September 3 – Mort Walker, American cartoonist (*Beetle Bailey*)
  - Glen Bell, American entrepreneur and founder of Taco Bell (d. 2010)
- September 6 – King Peter II of Yugoslavia (d. 1970)
- September 7 – Madeleine Dring, British composer and actress (d. 1977)

- September 9 – Daniel Carleton Gajdusek, American virologist, recipient of the Nobel Prize in Physiology or Medicine (d. 2008)
- September 11 – Vasilije Mokranjac, Serbian composer (d. 1984)
- September 16 – Lee Kuan Yew, Prime Minister of Singapore (d. 2015)
- September 17 – Hank Williams, American country musician (d. 1953)
- September 18 – Queen Anne of Romania
- September 20 – Geraldine Clinton Little, Irish-born poet (d. 1997)
- September 22 – Dannie Abse, Welsh poet (d. 2014)
- September 26 – Dev Anand, Legendary Indian actor, film producer, writer and director (d. 2011)

October

Charlton Heston

- October 2 – Eugenio Cruz Vargas, Chilean poet and painter (d. 2014)
- October 3 – Edward Oliver LeBlanc, Dominican politician (d. 2004)

- October 4 – Charlton Heston, American actor (*The Ten Commandments*) (d. 2008)
- October 5
  - Albert Guðmundsson, Icelandic professional football player and politician (d. 1994)
  - Glynis Johns, British actress
  - Ricardo Lavié, Argentine actor (d. 2010)
- October 6 – Yasar Kemal, Turkish writer (d. 2015)
- October 7 – Irma Grese, German Nazi war criminal (d. 1945)
- October 10
  - James "Jabby" Jabara, American aviator, the first American jet fighter ace (d. 1966)
  - Murray Walker, British motor racing commentator
- October 13 – Faas Wilkes, Dutch football (soccer) player (d. 2006)
- October 15 – Italo Calvino, Italian writer (d. 1985)
- October 17 – Charles McClendon, Hall of Fame college football coach (d. 2001)
- October 20 – Otfried Preußler, German children's books author (d. 2013)
- October 23 – Frank Sutton, American actor (d. 1974)
- October 24
  - Sir Robin Day, British political broadcaster (d. 2000)
  - Denise Levertov, British-born American poet (d. 1997)

- October 25 – J. Esmonde Barry, Canadian healthcare activist and political commentator (d. 2007)

Roy Lichtenstein

- October 27 – Roy Lichtenstein, American pop artist (d. 1997)
- October 29
    - Carl Djerassi, American chemist (d. 2015)
    - Gerda van der Kade-Koudijs, Dutch athlete (d. 2015)

November

Jack Kilby

Vicco von Bülow

- November 1
    - Victoria de los Ángeles, Catalan soprano (d. 2005)
    - Gordon R. Dickson, Canadian author (d. 2001)
- November 2 – Cesare Rubini, Italian basketball player and coach (d. 2011)
- November 3 – Tomás Cardinal Ó Fiaich, Irish Roman Catholic prelate (d. 1990)
- November 5
    - Rudolf Augstein, German journalist, founder and part-owner of German magazine Der Spiegel (d. 2002)
    - Kay Lionikas, Greek-American female professional baseball player (d. 1978)
- November 8 – Jack Kilby, American electrical engineer, recipient of the Nobel Prize in Physics (d. 2005)
- November 12 – Vicco von Bülow, German actor (d. 2011)
- November 13 – Linda Christian, Mexican film actress (d. 2011)

- November 17 – Aristides Maria Pereira, President of Cape Verde (d. 2011)
- November 18 – Alan Shepard, first American astronaut (d. 1998)
- November 20 – Nadine Gordimer, South African writer, Nobel Prize laureate (d. 2014)
- November 22 – Arthur Hiller, Canadian film director
- November 23
  - Billy Haughton, American harness driver and trainer (d. 1986)
  - Julien J. LeBourgeois, American vice admiral (d. 2012)
  - Gloria Whelan, American poet, short story writer, and novelist
- November 25 – Mauno Koivisto, President of Finland
- November 26 – Pat Phoenix, English actress (d. 1986)

December

Maria Callas

Bob Barker

- December 1 – Stansfield Turner, American admiral and Director of Central Intelligence
- December 2 – Maria Callas, Greek soprano (d. 1977)
- December 3
  - Dede Allen, American film editor ("Bonnie and Clyde") (d. 2010)
  - Moyra Fraser, British actress (d. 2009)
  - Abe Pollin, American sports owner (d. 2009)
- December 5 – Eleanor Dapkus, American female professional baseball player (d. 2011)
- December 5 – Philip Slier, Dutch Jewish typesetter (d. 1943)
- December 11 – Betsy Blair, American film actress (d. 2009)
- December 12 – Bob Barker, American game show host (*The Price Is Right*)
- December 13
  - Philip Warren Anderson, American physicist, Nobel Prize laureate
  - Larry Doby, baseball player (d. 2003)
  - Antoni Tàpies, Catalan painter (d. 2012)

- December 14
  - Gerard Reve, Dutch writer (d. 2006)
  - Sully Boyar, American actor (d. 2001)
- December 15 – Freeman Dyson, English-born physicist
- December 17 – Jaroslav Pelikan, American historian (d. 2006)
- December 19 – Gordon Jackson, Scottish actor (d. 1990)
- December 23
  - TL Osborn, American televangelist, singer and author (d. 2013)
  - James Stockdale, U.S. Navy admiral and vice presidential candidate (d. 2005)
- December 24 – George Patton IV, American general (d. 2004)
- December 25
  - Sonya Olschanezky, World War II heroine (d. 1944)
  - Satyananda Saraswati, Founder of Satyananda Yoga and Bihar Yoga (d. 2009)
  - René Girard, French-American historian (d. 2015)
- December 27 – Lucas Mangope, President of Bophuthatswana Bantustan
- December 29 – Dina Merrill, American actress, heiress, socialite, and philanthropist

Deaths

January–June

Wilhelm Röntgen

- January 1 – Willie Keeler, American baseball player and MLB Hall of Famer (b. 1872)
- January 3 – Jaroslav Hašek, Czech writer (b. 1883)
- January 9
  - Katherine Mansfield, English novelist (b. 1888)
  - Edith Thompson and Frederick Bywaters, English couple hanged for murder (Thompson b. 1893)
- January 11 – Constantine I of Greece, King of Greece (b. 1868)
- January 12 – Herbert Silberer, Austrian psychoanalyst (b. 1882)
- January 13 – Alexandre Ribot, French statesman, former Prime Minister (b. 1842)
- January 18 – Wallace Reid, American actor (b. 1891)
- January 23 – Max Nordau, Hungarian author, philosopher, and Zionist leader (b. 1849)

- January 31 – Eligiusz Niewiadomski, Polish artist, political activist and assassin (executed) (b. 1869)
- February 1 – Ernst Troeltsch, German theologian (b. 1865).
- February 3 – Count Kuroki Tamemoto, Japanese general (b. 1844)
- February 5 – Count Erich Kielmansegg, former Prime Minister of Austria (b. 1847)
- February 10 – Wilhelm Röntgen, German physicist, Nobel Prize laureate (b. 1845)
- February 23 – Théophile Delcassé, French statesman (b. 1852)
- March 8 – Johannes Diderik van der Waals, Dutch physicist, Nobel Prize laureate (b. 1837)
- March 26 – Sarah Bernhardt, French actress (b. 1844)
- March 27 – Sir James Dewar, Scottish chemist (b. 1842)
- March 28 – Michel-Joseph Maunoury, French general (b. 1847)
- April 4 – John Venn, British mathematician (b. 1834)
- April 5 – George Herbert, 5th Earl of Carnarvon, English financier of Egyptian excavations (b. 1866)
- April 23 – Princess Louise of Prussia, Grand Duchess of Baden (b. 1838)
- May 10 – Charles de Freycinet, four-time Prime Minister of France (b. 1828)
- May 21 – Hans Goldschmidt, German chemist (b. 1861)

Sarah Bernhardt

- May 29 – Albert Deullin, French flying ace of World War I (b. 1890)
- June 9 – Princess Helena of the United Kingdom, third daughter of Queen Victoria (b. 1846)
- June 10 – Pierre Loti, French writer and naval officer (b. 1850)
- June 14 – Isabelle Bogelot, French philanthropist (b. 1838)
- June 18 – Hristo Smirnenski, Bulgarian poet (b. 1898)
- June 24 – Edith Södergran, Finnish author (b. 1892)

July–December

Gustave Eiffel

- July 10 – Albert Chevalier, English music hall comedian (b. 1861)
- July 20 – Pancho Villa, Mexican revolutionary (assassinated) (b. 1878)

- July 23 – Charles Dupuy, French statesman, former Prime Minister (b. 1851)
- August 2 – Warren G. Harding, 29th President of the United States (b. 1865)
- August 10 – Joaquín Sorolla, Spanish painter (b. 1863)
- August 23 – Henry C. Mustin, American naval aviation pioneer (b. 1874)
- August 24 – Katō Tomosaburō, 21st Prime Minister of Japan (b. 1861)
- September 9 – Hermes Rodrigues da Fonseca, 8th President of Brazil (b. 1855)
- September 23
  - Carl L. Boeckmann, Norwegian-American artist (b. 1867)
  - John Morley, 1st Viscount Morley of Blackburn, British politician and editor (b. 1838)
- October 28
  - Theodor Reuss, German occultist (b. 1855)
  - Stojan Protić, Serbian statesman, former Prime Minister of Yugoslavia (b. 1857)
- October 30 – Andrew Bonar Law, Prime Minister of the United Kingdom (b. 1858)
- November 9 (among those killed in Munich Beer Hall Putsch):
  - Oskar Körner, businessman (b. 1875)
  - Karl Laforce, student (b. 1904)
  - Ludwig Maximilian Erwin von Scheubner-Richter, diplomat and revolutionary (b. 1884)

- November 14 – Ernest Augustus, Crown Prince of Hanover (b. 1845)
- November 15 – Mohammad Yaqub Khan, former Emir of Afghanistan (b. 1849)
- November 30 – Martha Mansfield, American actress (b. 1899)
- December 2 – Tomás Bretón, Spanish composer (b. 1850)
- December 8 – John William Brodie-Innes, British member of Golden Dawn (b. 1848)
- December 12 – Raymond Radiguet, French author (b. 1903)
- December 13 – Théophile Steinlen, Swiss painter (b. 1859)
- December 22 – Georg Luger, German firearms designer (b. 1849)
- December 27
  - Gustave Eiffel, French engineer and architect (Eiffel Tower) (b. 1832)
  - Lluís Domènech i Montaner, Spanish Catalan architect (b. 1850)

Date unknown

- Edmund William Berridge, British medical doctor (b. 1843)
- Dorila Antommarchi, Colombian poet (b. 1850s)

Nobel Prizes

- Physics – Robert Andrews Millikan
- Chemistry – Fritz Pregl
- Physiology or Medicine – Frederick Grant Banting,
- John James Rickard Macleod
- Literature – William Butler Yeats

In the News

Women's One Piece swimming suits begin to be worn.

Mount Etna volcano erupts on June 19th.

King Tutankhamun's Burial Chamber opened by Howard Carter.

The Great Kanto earthquake devastate the cities of Tokyo and Yokohama.

Construction starts on the Sydney Harbor Bridge.

The worlds first domestic **refrigerator** is sold in Sweden.

First Le Mans 24 hour race run in France.

1923 Calendar

January 1923
Sun	Mon	Tue	Wed	Thu	Fri	Sat
	1	2	3	4	5	6
7	8	9	10	11	12	13
14	15	16	17	18	19	20
21	22	23	24	25	26	27
28	29	30	31			

February 1923
Sun	Mon	Tue	Wed	Thu	Fri	Sat
				1	2	3
4	5	6	7	8	9	10
11	12	13	14	15	16	17
18	19	20	21	22	23	24
25	26	27	28			

March 1923
Sun	Mon	Tue	Wed	Thu	Fri	Sat
				1	2	3
4	5	6	7	8	9	10
11	12	13	14	15	16	17
18	19	20	21	22	23	24
25	26	27	28	29	30	31

April 1923
Sun	Mon	Tue	Wed	Thu	Fri	Sat
1	2	3	4	5	6	7
8	9	10	11	12	13	14
15	16	17	18	19	20	21
22	23	24	25	26	27	28
29	30					

May 1923
Sun	Mon	Tue	Wed	Thu	Fri	Sat
		1	2	3	4	5
6	7	8	9	10	11	12
13	14	15	16	17	18	19
20	21	22	23	24	25	26
27	28	29	30	31		

June 1923
Sun	Mon	Tue	Wed	Thu	Fri	Sat
					1	2
3	4	5	6	7	8	9
10	11	12	13	14	15	16
17	18	19	20	21	22	23
24	25	26	27	28	29	30

July 1923
Sun	Mon	Tue	Wed	Thu	Fri	Sat
1	2	3	4	5	6	7
8	9	10	11	12	13	14
15	16	17	18	19	20	21
22	23	24	25	26	27	28
29	30	31				

August 1923
Sun	Mon	Tue	Wed	Thu	Fri	Sat
			1	2	3	4
5	6	7	8	9	10	11
12	13	14	15	16	17	18
19	20	21	22	23	24	25
26	27	28	29	30	31	

September 1923
Sun	Mon	Tue	Wed	Thu	Fri	Sat
						1
2	3	4	5	6	7	8
9	10	11	12	13	14	15
16	17	18	19	20	21	22
23	24	25	26	27	28	29
30						

October 1923
Sun	Mon	Tue	Wed	Thu	Fri	Sat
	1	2	3	4	5	6
7	8	9	10	11	12	13
14	15	16	17	18	19	20
21	22	23	24	25	26	27
28	29	30	31			

November 1923
Sun	Mon	Tue	Wed	Thu	Fri	Sat
				1	2	3
4	5	6	7	8	9	10
11	12	13	14	15	16	17
18	19	20	21	22	23	24
25	26	27	28	29	30	

December 1923
Sun	Mon	Tue	Wed	Thu	Fri	Sat
						1
2	3	4	5	6	7	8
9	10	11	12	13	14	15
16	17	18	19	20	21	22
23	24	25	26	27	28	29
30	31